Word Vomit

Maysa Sarkis

Presentation by *BookLeaf Publishing*

Web: www.bookleafpub.com

E-mail: info@bookleafpub.com

ISBN: 9789357212984

First edition 2023

For Mum - my biggest supporter.

*She started me on reading and has been
reading my creative drafts since the beginning
<3*

ACKNOWLEDGEMENT

As my first published book I feel like there is a lot of people to thank, and I am worried I will forget them all.

I always feared rejection, so dealing with constructive criticism was always heartbreaking, but thank you to those who dealt with my breakdowns and actually helped me improve my work.

Thank you to all of those who have always encouraged me to continue writing. Reminding me that I actually need to start something and have people read it, if wanted a chance to be an author. Reminding me that I am my own harshest critic, and my works are better than I think. Reminding me to enjoy myself when doing this because it should be for fun.

Thank you
My Family
My Friends (aka yo rent a house)
My Boyfriend
My Teachers (both in High school and University)

For helping me blossom into the writer I am today

And you, dear reader, thanks for choosing to give me a chance.

PREFACE

The majority of these poems have been sitting in my notes app for ages - I have been too afraid to let them see the light.

A few have been posted by myself to social media, but today is a big day.
The first time I will be debuting my writing on print.

Being able to hold onto such precious words and see others celebrate them is so surreal, and I hope I am able to continue doing this for years to come.

Enjoy!
And please reach out to me on facebook if you want to chat about writing :)

Swimming Lessons

Somedays I wake up in a pool
And when I realise what's happening
I begin to drown

Somedays people come by and just watch
Or
They'll point and laugh

Other days some pour more water,
feeding the pool
Or
They just grab my head,
and push me deeper

But one day someone tried to drain it

They dove underwater
And tried to pull the plug
Freeing the water
But it was too rusted over; stuck.

That did not stop them

They grabbed buckets
Emptying the pool manually

Scoop it up and Pour it out.
I thought they'd tire out
But they were so determined.

I was no longer drowning
My feet could touch the pool floor
But oddly enough, they didn't get out of the pool
and leave
Instead,
They started to teach me how to tread water.
Softly kicking my legs, so I could fight the water
incase it rose again.

And then
Once I could do that
They also taught me how to swim

So,
When I wake up in the pool
I am no longer drowning

My False Prophet

You were my false prophet

A dimming halo

Faded white

Molting wings

You were my false prophet

Matted hair

Torn dress

An untuned harp

You were my false prophet

Saccharine serenades spilled out of chapped lips

Your guiding hand, cold and clammy

Eyes brimming with tears with every request

You were my false prophet

I accepted

I indulged

I paid the price

Trying to Start Again Hurts but It's Necessary

It took more than a step in the right direction.
More like a push, or a shove, no actually a kick.

Sealed windows. No bursts of fresh air in or out.
Just the stench of staleness.
Lights out. Just darkness. All encroaching, all
consuming.
Growing piles of… things…. You couldn't even
name them, just random little objects. There
were no such things as hidden corners, with new
junk forcing itself into any space it could. It was
crowded, cluttered chaos.

All I did was sleep. Dipping my toes into death's
domain for as many hours as I could. Fading fast
then jerking awake with burning eyes and a dry
throat. Repeat that four times a day and you
have the routine of the god's.

With fungus for hair and slime for skin,
cocooned in weeks-old bedsheets that only smelt
good as I doused them in cheap perfume, I
would emerge from my execution chamber for
three key reasons:

1. To Land knees first in a heap in-front of the porcelain throne where I'd begin to sweat. And then, begin to retch. It was a chunky, bitter barf-stew.
2. To release the clogging waste of my insides.
3. To make a pit-stop at the dwindling kitchen-cupboard and steal a cracker to nibble on like a yearning rat.

Every so often, I'd check my phone.
Questions, memories from the pasts and plights of pity.

It wasn't worth it.
It was never worth it.

Until I saw you cry.

Eyes brimming with regrets and worry; wondering where you went wrong and desperate to do anything to heave your daughter out of the melting-pot of depression.

Thats when I cried too. Stumbling, tumbling, fumbling into your arms and wailing until I couldn't anymore. Screams of anguish filling the house like the cries of a dying fox. And you just stood there, gripping onto me and not letting go.

I drenched your shirt so heavily we ending up
chucking it out.

I made so many promises that night; swearing to
any god that would listen I wouldn't let it
happen again.
The first one I achieved was having a
well-needed shower; scrubbing and scraping off
layers of grime and despair.

My bedside-table slowly became a chemist.
Home to pill-packets and self-help books. I
actually liked it.

I took your hand and began to book as many
appointments, they swore this was normal and
things would change - "get better".

That was two years ago.

Now I'm leaning against the bathroom sink, hair
combed back and a dazzling in a brand new
dress. I start the process of brushing my teeth.
Rinse my mouth out. Repeat at least three times.
Glob of minty fresh teeth whitening toothpaste
on a faded pink toothbrush. Hard and fast
movements starting from the back and working
to the front. My eyes catch the mirror, and all I
see is a dog sick with rabies.

I begin to giggle.

Small, stupid moments like that made life worth
it.

Numb

249 unread notifications
12 missed calls
8 overdue reminders
And I still don't care

15 unexplained absences
9 late fees
7 missing assignments
And I still don't care

4 months sleeping in unwashed linen
3 weeks of skipping showers
2 days where I didn't brush my teeth
And I still don't care

The pit is growing
deeper;

A vacuous black hole
Ever consuming
Ever accepting

A place I'll never leave

You've Got Mail!

I've written you a thousand letters
All of which I'll never send
Each a variation of the same story
Questioning that never ends

The Otherside

Contrary to popular belief, remembering the moment you saw the ghost of your dead Grandma is a very difficult thing to do.

Memories are foggy little things that get caught on specifics, like a jacket catching on a doorknob as one tries to hurry away. I can remember that the soul (no)…vision (no)…ghost (no)…Grandma wore a purple, pleated sweater with fraying hems. And that her pants were grey and a tad too short so they curled around her ankles. And even the flimsy black slippers she wore over her swollen feet is etched into my mind.

And I can remember that she had no eyes.

All she had were golf-ball sized, black abysses. There weren't any gorey details, like her eyes had been forcefully ripped out of her skull or in her old age her eyes shrivelled up and fell out; there was just a blank slate, emptiness, nothingness, clear space that was so obviously meant to be filled.

Dreams of those eyeless holes plagued my feeble brain for weeks. The two voids easily followed my every movement. The unending craters could swallow you up in one quick gulp. I could be walking through a crowd and she'd be there - her silver bouncy bob framing her gaunt face. Her veins, tiny blue spider-webs, spindling across her cheeks. Dry chapped lips, covered in flaking lipstick, that remained pursed. And still no eyes.

But, at the end of the day, I can't remember what she said or why she was there or what I did either. That's shared through casual laughs on Halloween night when everyone wants a shiver sent down their spine or during mandatory, introductory trivia games because I have always wanted to be an unique little attention-grabber.

It goes a little something like this:

September. Springtime. 2009. Aged six with beet-red cheeks, the voice of a squeak-toy and without a care in the world.

Two days prior, I had been dragged to Hospital to say goodbye to my Grandma. She was sick. She was dying. I didn't actually know what that meant. I was too worried that my mum would

cry when I asked her. My Dad told me it was
like a permanent holiday. He's lucky I did not go
around telling everyone I wanted to die just like
Grandma.

The night it happened I came screaming down
the hallway; my chubby legs plodding fast and
loud, my uncle mistook it for an Earthquake.

My Dads on the phone with Mum.
"She's Gone".

I look at him with tears hotly rolling down
questioning why grammy's in my room wishing
me well and saying goodbye.

And only silence responds.

House

The sun beat down on the small, unlikely group of six girls, each in casually mismatched outfits. A checkered picnic blanket laid haphazardly on the ground, with muddy shoes piled in each of the four corners to stop it from moving. Strewn across were piles of half eaten foods - sweets, pizza, rice, chips, crackers, cheeses, fruit, cans of fizzy - they had overbought; like always. The wind occasionally picked up speed, whipping their tied hair and letting leaves hover off the ground before lightly floating back down. The grass was tall and thick and it made them itch, but their loud laughter and excited shoving showed no indication of discomfort. The cries of little kids throwing rubber balls at each other, running around without a care in the world, was background music to their conversation.

I remember it all too well.
I want to go back, freeze myself in that spot, the celebratory picnic in the park - claiming the only tree on the hill.

Impetigo

I can't stop itching

Crusting red dots demand attention
I swear there was only one a minute ago
They pop up with vigour and refuse to leave;
like a drunken guest who doesn't know when to
go home
My hands sneak to the spot with a mind of their
own
It starts with a slow rub; I'm not scratching I'm
massaging the itch - it's safer
And then the hook of the nail grazes the surface

And all hell breaks loose

And I just make it worse

I pick
I poke
I prod
Letting my nails destroy the dot

Till I bleed

Termination

My life has been pushed and pulled into a
million strands; a chaotic cacophony. Messily
stretched thin. A piece for everyone. I'm always
going back and forth, back and forth, back and
forth. Constantly swinging - never stuck in the
mud or a one track mind.

You were the only constant.

My home.

At my side in a moments' notice; slipping your
hand into mine and whispering promises into my
ear - pouring yourself into me.
I know now those promises were simply a
façade of everything I've ever wanted. You were
extending your cruel hand forward, begging me
to take it, and I did. It took a while, but when
you could, you plunged that hand into my chest
and locked a vice grip onto my heart. Even
today my chest still tightens and your hands
remain bloody.

Every time I was around you a hum of electricity jolted my system, a warm buzz bubbling under my skin, ready to spill out. I was pulled into your warmth, ready to risk burning for you - letting my skin melt and drip down into a puddle on the concrete floor, becoming red raw with a thousand blisters ready to pop at a moment's notice. It was always anything for you.

It was so good, greater than good. An indescribable cycle of excitement I was caught up in. Cherishing every part of you that I forgot myself. Offering every part of me to be sacrificed for you. A worshipper at your feet, a tool to be used.
A
   soar
       crackle
           bang
              in my heart.
Until it wasn't.

Suddenly pushed away, tossed aside. Told everything was a lie.

Hallelujah

Who shall I become; the preacher or the son?

Let the numb succumb
To begging for the grace of the saviours touch

And they will bathe in the blessed blood
of the cursed hearts

I ignore the call
And forge my own path

Emotional Dysregulation

Anger seeps out of my skin and heats the floor
underneath me
It follows me like a fog
A thunderous roar

I spit fire
Saying things I don't mean
Going for the jugular

And then their lip quivers
And then their eyes steel
And then they run away
And then I know I messed up

Him

It's embarrassing to admit your in love.

But I can't help it when I'm with him

There are so many things I want to say.
I stare at him and cannot look away.

I know everything about him.
His obsession with cars.
His dedication to family life.
His fear of bugs.
His dreams
His nightmares

But when he sends me that soft smile,
The words die in my throat
And all I can do is smile back.

My body tingles and I'm a giddy school girl.
Biting my lip, covering my face, kicking my
legs.

I hope he knows

I hope he knows it all

All the unsaid words

How lucky I am to have him
How grateful I am for him
How he really did save me.

But he also needs to know,
How beautiful he is.

That I love how his hair is as curly as the fur of
poodles.
And when it wraps around the nape of his neck
as he tries to tame it.

That I love how his cheeks are plump and round
like a squirrel storing nuts.

That I love his strength
emotionally and physically
He can pick me up with ease; slinging me over
his shoulder like a prize.
No one has ever been able to do that before.
More importantly
He cries in front of me
He voices his worries
He forgives
He comforts

There's a kindness in him you cannot find
elsewhere.
One that I wish I had myself.
He bares his true soul
And doesn't care about the consequences.

That I love his voice
even if he hates it -
It's actually the one thing that always changing
about him
When he's tired its' deep and gravelly
When excited, boisterous and bubbly

He's laying down next to me right now.
Eyes fluttering shut but murmuring he won't fall
asleep (he will).
I shuffle closer to him,
letting his hands wrap around my waist and
feeling him nuzzle into my back.

I am complete.

20mg Citalopram Daily

Sitting on the old train, You stare blankly out the
window, forehead pressed up against the glass.
Your tinged cheeks vibrate along with the
movement of the carriage. Distraction. That's
what You craves as You attempts to transfix
Your eyes on the passing blurred masses.

That does not work!

Rubbing your clammy hands against the ruffles
of your skirt, pretending to smoothen the
non-existence creases rather than reveal the
sweat accumulating on those small palms, you
fidget in the cold steel seat. It felt so refreshing
against the slivers of uncovered skin but a
nagging thought crept into your mind that you'd
leave a sweaty little ass print on the seat - gross -
better not get too comfortable.

You leaned forward - elbows now on knees -
cursing god for it being a 40 degree day, the first
time you gain the courage to take public
transport.

You are hyperaware of everything.

It's gnawing at the back of Your brain
You cannot shake it

Its happening again

Why must this dread that always simmered in
your belly, bubble to your lips and spill out
harshly.

....
.....
....
....

You lost

Connected

We are coils of DNA;
intrinsically intertwined;
inseparable and
interdependent.

My existence hinges on yours.

You are the feral cat with radioactive eyes
Scrutinising all as you whip your head from left
to right and then left again
Sashaying your tail
Skilfully skirting around machinery
Jumping onto empty ledges
Then hissing. loudly.
Forcing me into the role of the mutt that chases
after.

And when our bodies finally interlock
It's a mirror image.

Both just scared little kids haunted by their
memories

sick

i am sick

sick in the head

sick in the stomach

sick of the world

sick of myself

sicksicksicksicksicksicksicksicksicksicksicksick
sicksicksicksicksicksicksick

Alone

I was the re-gifted present.

The last slice of cake offered to every guest yet
they're too full or too modest to claim

Every ball in every fucking sport; passed
around, thrown between zones

A floater

Never belonging

Never tied down

I used to celebrate my independence

But now I know it was a mask

A fragile husk of my lonely reality

No Supporter
No Friend
No Lover

Completely And Utterly I S O L A T E D

Missing Someone You Shouldn't

I don't miss you.

I don't miss the way your face flushed and you'd
shove me when I'd tell you you're beautiful.
I don't miss your encouraging words whenever
I'm down.
I don't miss the way you'd lay your head in my
lap, no matter where we were.
I don't miss the way your eyebrows quirked
when you said something silly.
I don't miss that laugh; a twinkling tune on
repeat.
I don't miss the constant updates you sent me.
Even now as I write this - a blinking beep on my
brick I call a phone; It's a picture of you I will
myself to discard.
I don't miss those eyes.
I don't miss running my fingers through your
frizzy hair.
I don't miss you linking our arms together.
I don't miss the purposefully over-exaggerated
kisses on the cheek which felt like I was covered
in dog slobber afterwards.

I don't miss the way you'd squeeze my sides
when we'd hug.

I don't miss you.

But I do.

When it's the middle of the night and I should be
asleep, I miss you.
When I hear your favourite song, I miss you.
And when I skip your posts online, I miss you.

Come home.

Enigma

5. She sits up straight, forcing herself to remember to keep up her posture. She absentmindedly picks at her nails, probably a habit she picked up when she was younger. Her eyes flitting between every movement they capture, her left leg bouncing up and down rhythmically. Perhaps she's overexcited, about to burst - or just a bundle of nerves?

4. Dark chocolate hair hangs low below her bottom, curling up at the ends. Her neon sweater, a beacon that draws you in. She wears big, bold earrings - a call to be noticed.

3. Although she's filled with questions, her own answers stay locked within. No one will crack her.

2. She swallows a witty retort; its much more importance to keep up appearances than start another fight.

1. She's the enigma.

Procrastination

Cocooned under the thicket of my blue blanket I
ignore my laptop and peer through a window.

Birds.

There are so many birds.

A rooster cries in the distance.
It's grating and guttural.
A rude reminder to break your stupor and
continue with the task at hand.

A pigeon and a rainbow lorikeet guard opposing
sides of the vegetable garden. Nothing is ready
to harvest but still they comfortably nestle into
it, the overgrown weeds a blanket as both birds
peck, peck, peck around.
Are they battling for food or resources?

The rainbow lorikeet drags its beak through the
surface of the dirt, never digging deeper into the
unknowingness of the rich soil.
It chucks twigs behind them, looking for
something else, something larger.

The pigeon is riskier.
Shoving their head straight down - any harder
I'd swear the bird would have given itself a
concussion (medically, can that actually
happen?).
The pigeon stills.
Suddenly, they're whipping back and hopping
around with a wriggling catch between their
beak.
The pigeon soars into the air, targeting the
closest tree.
It is forgotten and old, curled scraps of bark
peeling down its' sides.
Still its' leaves stood proud - emeralds swishing
as the pigeon hides between them, chowing
down on its prize.

The rainbow lorikeet's beady pools of black
stare up longingly at the pigeon.
They tut
and
fly
away.

Goodnight

The moon cried as the stars dimmed to black.